HOW TO BUILD A SKYSCRAPER

by Jilly Hunt
Illustrated by Victor Medina

Contents

What Are Skyscrapers?	2
Learning from the Past	4
Careful Construction	6
New Materials	8
Careful Design	12
Dig Down to Build Up	14
Building the Superstructure	16
Adding the Outer Wall	18
Crucial Technology	20
The Growth of Skyscrapers	22
Glossary and Index	24

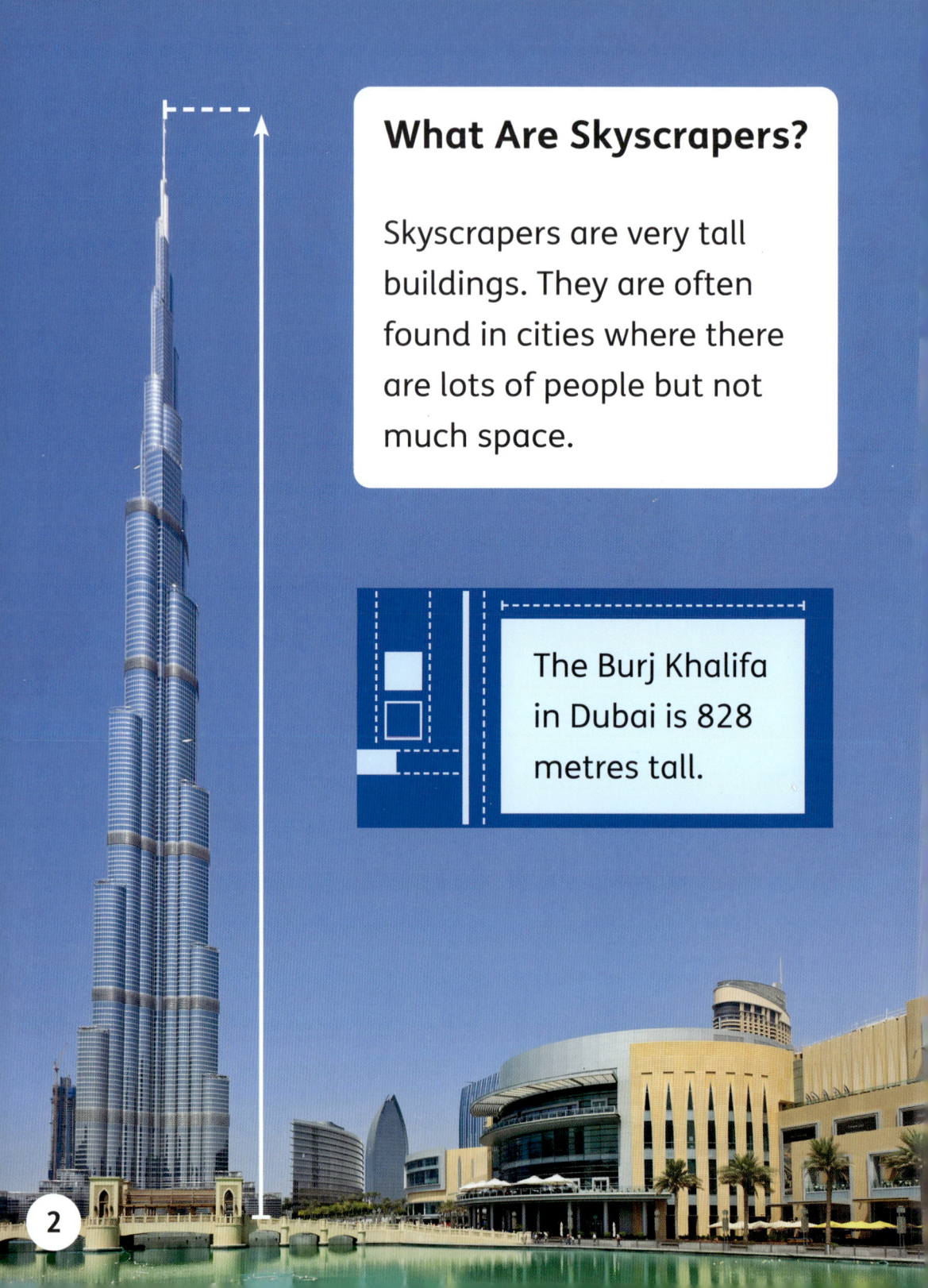

What Are Skyscrapers?

Skyscrapers are very tall buildings. They are often found in cities where there are lots of people but not much space.

The Burj Khalifa in Dubai is 828 metres tall.

Architects build models to help <u>prove</u> that their designs for skyscrapers will work.

Architects need to <u>prove</u> their buildings will work. Why do you think it's important to <u>prove</u> that tall buildings won't fall down?

Learning from the Past

The Ancient Egyptian pyramids were the first skyscrapers ever built. They were once the tallest buildings in the world.

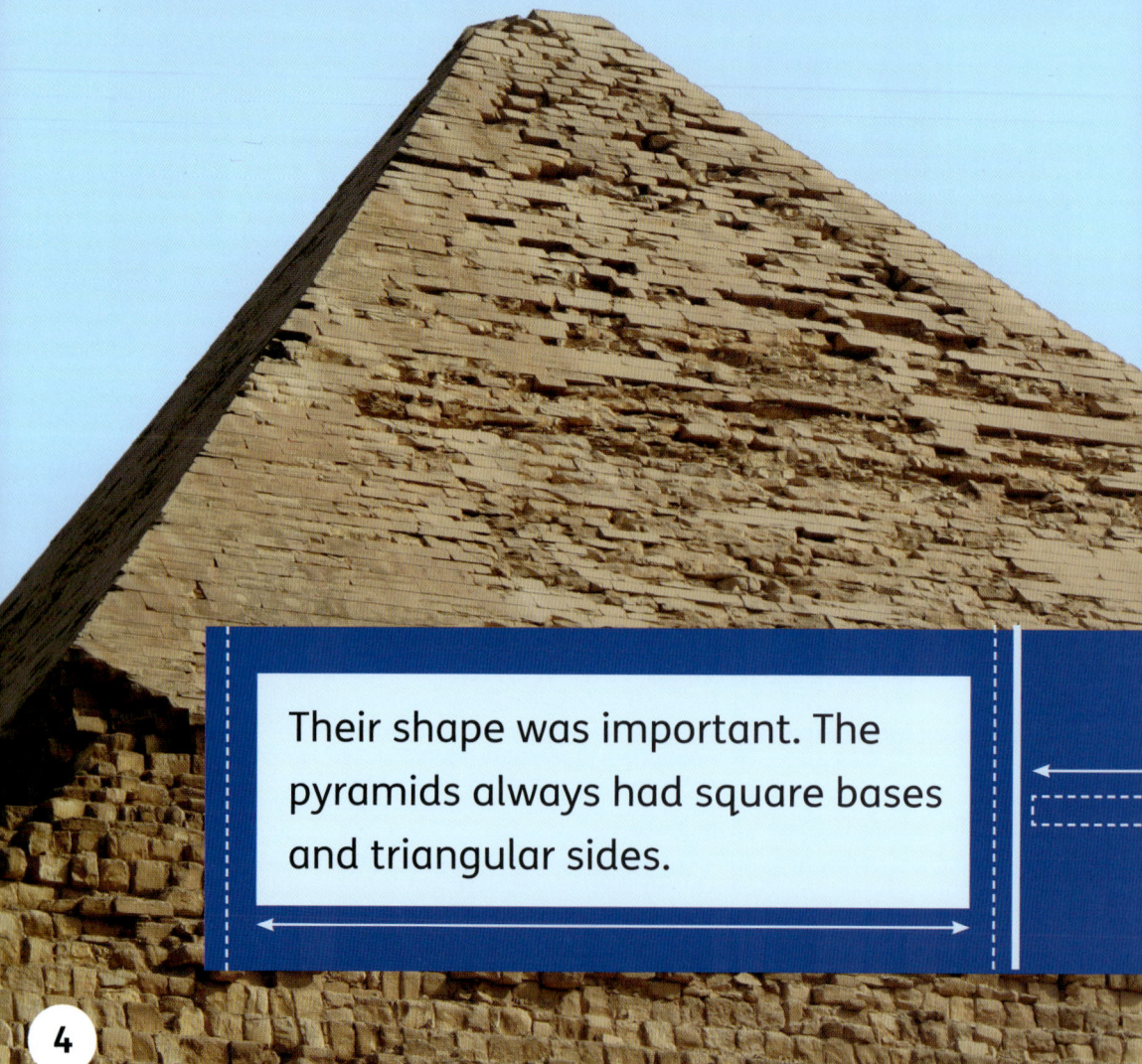

Their shape was important. The pyramids always had square bases and triangular sides.

BUILD IT!

Find out which shape is the strongest.

You will need:
- spaghetti
- modelling clay.

Method

1. Join strands of spaghetti with balls of modelling clay to make a triangle and a rectangle.

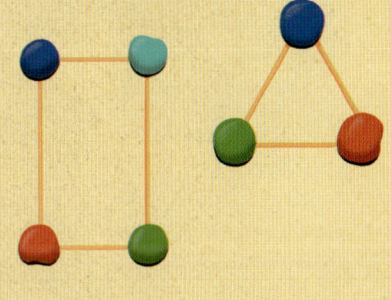

2. Hold the rectangle upright. What happens if you push on one of the top corners?

3. Now hold the triangle upright. Push down on the top. What happens?

Which shape was the strongest?

Careful Construction

The Great Pyramid of Giza was about 147 metres tall when it was built. It was made from over 2 300 000 **limestone** blocks.

Each block weighs about 2 500 kilograms … that's heavier than a rhinoceros!

The Egyptians didn't have modern machines to help them build the Great Pyramid. <u>Somehow</u> they managed to fit all these blocks together. There are many different ideas about how they did this, but it is still a mystery!

<u>Somehow</u> means in some way. Has the author used the word <u>somehow</u> because we know exactly how the blocks were fitted together or because we're not quite sure?

New Materials

Over time, people made stronger building materials. The stronger materials could support more weight. This meant that buildings could be taller. At first, iron and bricks were used. Then people used steel, which was lighter and stronger.

The first skyscraper was only ten **storeys** high.

Some materials are strong and can support heavy weight. What does support mean here? Can you think of any other words to use instead of support?

Table of properties

Metal	Properties
Iron	hard but breaks easily
Wrought iron	can easily be made into different shapes
Steel	strong and lightweight

BUILD IT!

Which materials will make the strongest model skyscraper?

You will need:
- A5 paper (cut into a ruler shape)
- A5 card (cut into a ruler shape)
- metal ruler
- plastic ruler
- a big clip
- sticky tape
- string
- a small pot
- weights.

Method

1. Use sticky tape to fix the paper, card, metal ruler and plastic ruler to the edge of a table.

2. Attach the big clip to the pot with the string and sticky tape.

3. Clip the pot on to the paper.

4. Add weights to the pot. What happens?

5. Repeat the test with all the other materials.

Careful Design

Architects and **engineers** need to carefully consider the design of skyscrapers. These tall buildings are very heavy. They must be designed so that the weight doesn't make them fall down.

The Gherkin in London weighs 10 000 tonnes.

Consider means to think carefully about something. When have you had to consider something carefully?

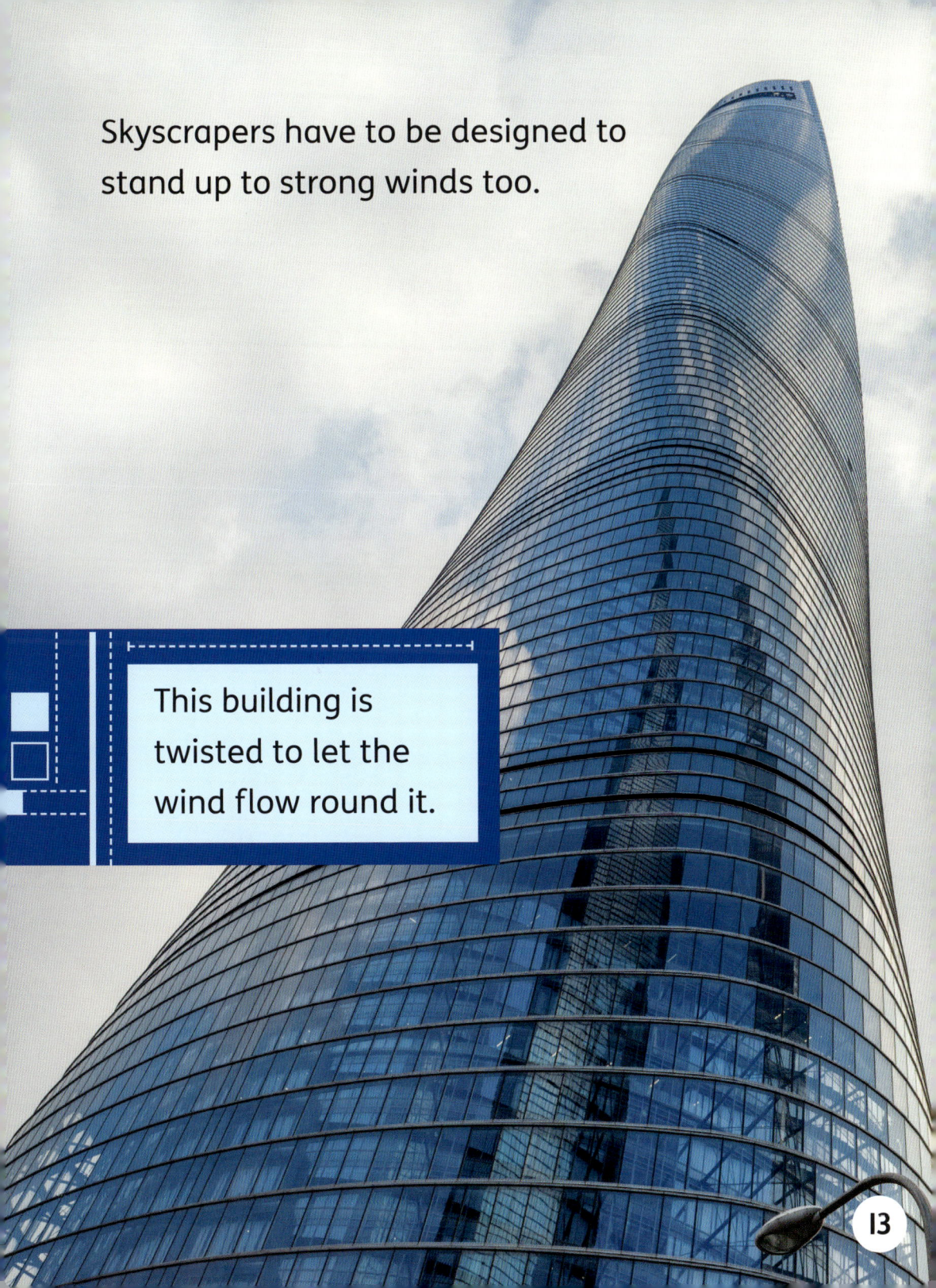

Skyscrapers have to be designed to stand up to strong winds too.

This building is twisted to let the wind flow round it.

Dig Down to Build Up

The first job in building a skyscraper is to make a base called a **foundation**. For lots of skyscrapers, this means digging a big hole.

The foundations have to be very strong. This is because the weight of the skyscraper pushes down on them with a lot of pressure.

Can you apply a gentle, steady pressure to this page with your finger?

Building the Superstructure

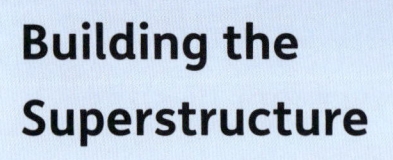

A steel frame is built on the foundations. This supports each floor of the skyscraper. It is often covered in **concrete**. The steel frame is called the superstructure.

frame

All the weight of a skyscraper goes through the frame.

Can you cover this page with something?

BUILD IT!

Find out which frame is strongest.

You will need:
- 16 lollipop sticks
- modelling clay
- a pile of books.

Method

1. Make a cube out of lollipop sticks and clay. How many books will it support?

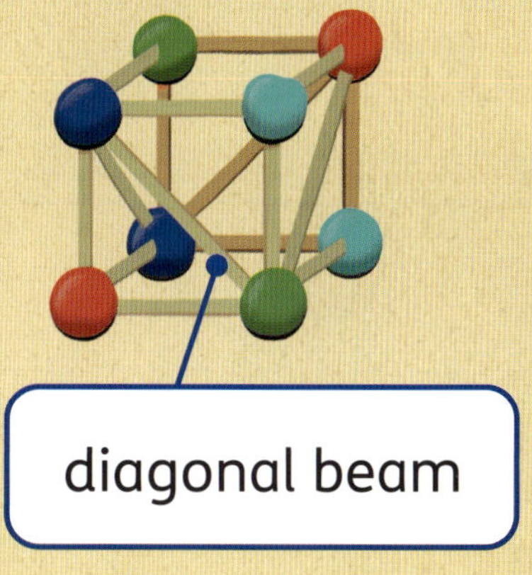

2. Add diagonal beams between the corners on each face. How many books can you add now?

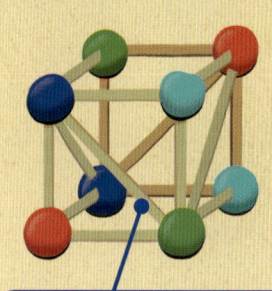

diagonal beam

Which of the two cubes in the pictures do you think will support the most books? Why?

Adding the Outer Wall

The outer wall of a skyscraper doesn't need to support the weight of the building. This means that architects can cover skyscrapers in thin materials like glass.

Huge glass windows can give you amazing views.

Teamwork

To build a skyscraper you need successful teamwork. Everyone needs to help each other to get the job done.

Crucial Technology

Skyscrapers would not be possible without some key inventions. Lifts, or elevators, were invented over 150 years ago.

This advert is for an early lift.

Cranes are another key invention. They are used to put up the frame of a skyscraper.

self-climbing crane

Self-climbing cranes move higher up the building as each new level is built.

The Growth of Skyscrapers

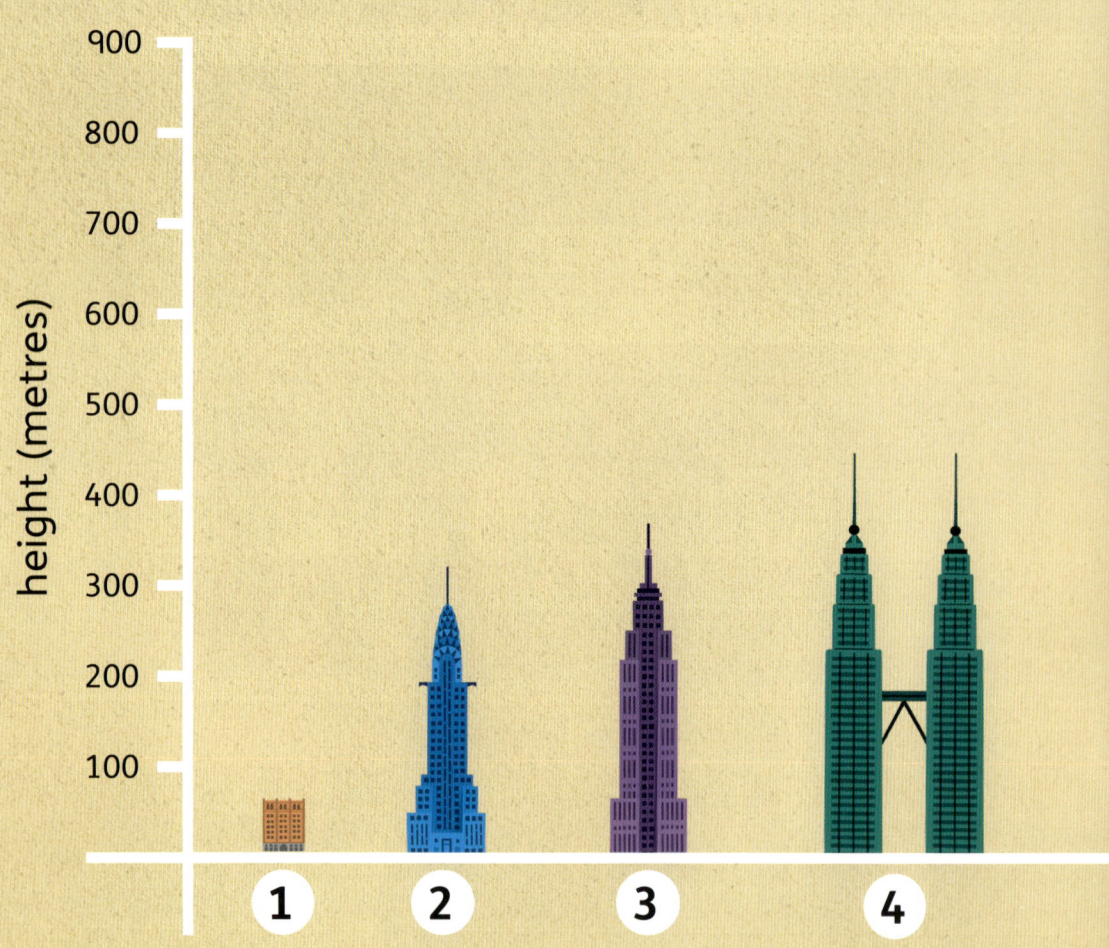

1. 1884–85: Home Insurance Building, Chicago
2. 1930: Chrysler Building, New York
3. 1931: Empire State Building, New York
4. 1998: Petronas Towers, Kuala Lumpur

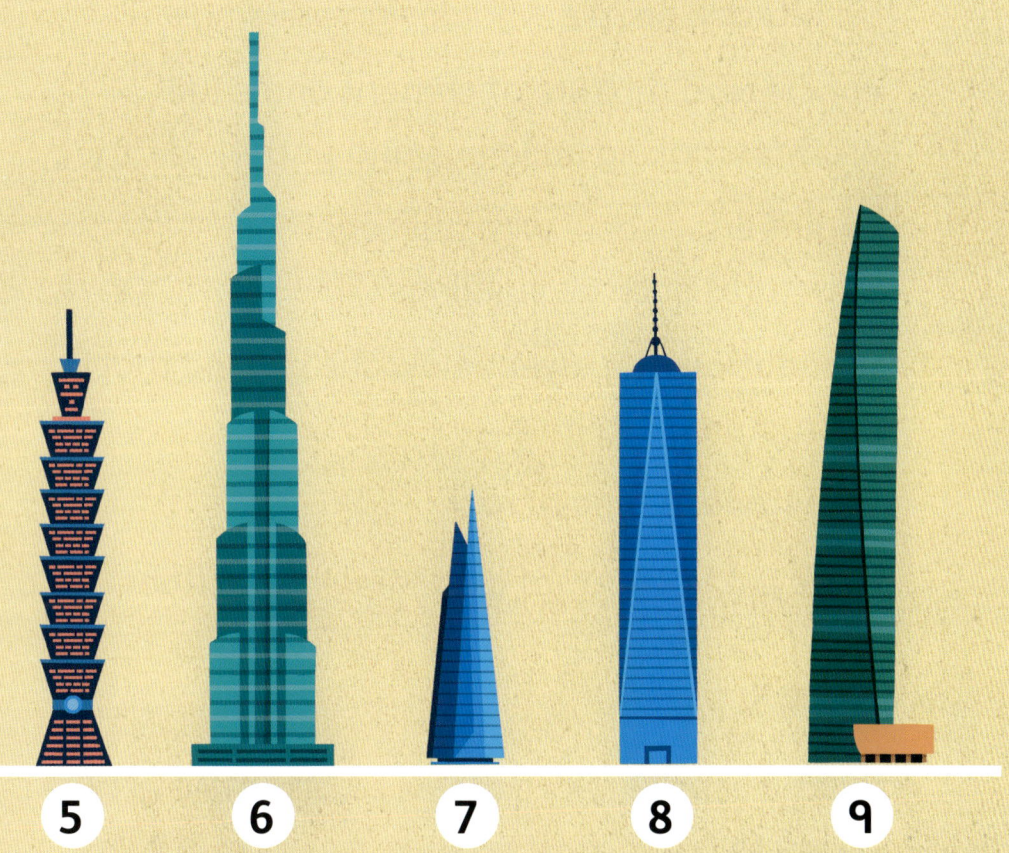

5 2004: Taipei 101, Taipei
6 2010: Burj Khalifa, Dubai
7 2013: The Shard, London
8 2014: One World Trade Center, New York
9 2015: Shanghai Tower, Shanghai

Glossary

architects: people who design buildings

concrete: a mixture of cement and sand used for making buildings and paths

engineers: people who put together structures such as buildings

foundation: the layer below the ground that a structure is built on

limestone: a type of rock

storey: one storey of a building is one floor

Index

Build It	5, 10–11, 17
concrete	14–15, 16
glass	18
iron	8, 9
pyramids	4, 6–7
steel	8, 9, 16